DATE DUE	

science@work
Food

PEPPERS, Popcorn, AND PIZZA

By Celeste A. Peters

RSVP

RAINTREE
STECK-VAUGHN
P U B L I S H E R S
A Steck-Vaughn Company

Austin, Texas

www.steck-vaughn.com

Published by Raintree Steck-Vaughn, an imprint of Steck-Vaughn Company

Library of Congress Cataloging-in-Publication Data

Peters, Celeste A. (Celeste Andra), 1953–
    Peppers, popcorn, and pizza: the science of food /
  by Celeste A. Peters
        p.   cm. — (Science [at] work)
  In ser. statement "[at]" appears as the at symbol.
  Includes bibliographical references and index.
  Summary: Introduces the scientific aspects of food, including how the body uses food as fuel, how each food has its own taste, and how to keep food fresh.
  ISBN 0-7398-0136-8
  1. Food—Juvenile literature. 2. Nutrition—Juvenile literature.
[1. Food. 2. Nutrition.] I. Title. II. Series: Science [at] work (Austin, Tex.)
TX355.P38   1999
641.3—dc21   99-10179
                                          CIP

Printed and bound in Canada
1 2 3 4 5 6 7 8 9 0   03 02 01 00 99

Project Coordinator
Ann Sullivan
Content Validator
Lois Edwards
Design
Warren Clark
Copy Editors
Rennay Craats
Elizabeth Entrup
Leslie Strudwick
Layout and Illustrations
Chantelle Sales
Photograph Credits
Every reasonable effort has been made to trace ownership and to obtain permission to reprint copyright material. The publishers would be pleased to have any errors or omissions brought to their attention so that they may be corrected in subsequent printings.

Dr. Terrence Beveridge (University of Guelph): page 18; **Corel Corporation**: cover background, left, page 4 top, bottom, 5 top left, 6, 7 top, 8, 9, 10 top, 12, 14, 19, 21, 22 top, 23, 24 left, 25, 28 right, 29 bottom, 30, 32, 33 top, 34 top, 35 top, bottom right, 36 bottom, 37 top, 38, 41, 42, 43; **Eyewire Incorporated**: page 35 bottom left, 40; **Michael McPhee**: page 28 left, 29 top, left; **National Aeronautics and Space Administration**: page 39; **Sharp Electronics Corporation**: page 27; **Tom Stack and Associates**: pages 4 middle, 7 bottom, 11 top (Brian Parker), 11 bottom, 37 bottom (Thomas Kitchin), 22 bottom (David M. Dennis), 31 (Inga Spence); **Trym Gym (University of Calgary)**: page 20; **Visuals Unlimited**: cover bottom right (Bud Nielsen), pages 13 (D. Yeske), 24 top (Bill Kamin), 26 (Bernd Wittich), 33 bottom (Mark E. Gibson), 34 left (A.J. Copley), 36 top (Jack M. Bostrack).

18749

Contents
....

Have you ever been hungry enough to "eat a horse"?

What about a snail or a beaver's tail?

What counts as food? A snail may not be your idea of a tasty snack, but it is a real treat for some people. Everyone needs food to survive, no matter what form it comes in. Food is the source of energy that keeps you going. Every mouthful of food is like a tiny battery pack! In addition to energy, food supplies the building blocks, such as proteins and nutrients, that your body uses to repair itself. Cooks know how to make food taste good and look mouthwatering. But which foods are best for you? You can find out by reading about nutrition, the science of food.

FINDING LINKS

Society

Small towns popped up around the world when our ancestors settled down to grow food crops. Today enough food to feed thousands of people is shipped to markets every day. This makes it possible for many people to live together in enormous cities.

Careers

Food is so important that there are thousands of jobs that involve growing, harvesting, selling, preparing, cooking, or serving food. Farmers, bakers, nutritionists, cooks, and restaurant owners are examples of people working in food-related careers.

Technology

From fire pits to microwave ovens, people have invented many ways to prepare, cook, and store food. Now our challenge is to invent ways to grow, cook, and eat food in outer space.

The Environment

Can you imagine growing banana plants at the North Pole or having a fish ranch in the middle of a desert? No! Plants and animals survive only where the climate, soil conditions, and amount of available water are right. We have changed the environment in some places to make it better able to grow food.

Our Energy Source

"Are there any snacks in the house?"

What is the first thing you do when you get home from school? Grab something to eat? You likely feel tired and need a "pick-me-up." Deep inside you know that a snack will give you the energy to play baseball, practice piano, or do homework until it is time for dinner. All animals, including humans, require food in order to keep going. Food provides the energy to move, breathe, and think clearly. If our energy source suddenly disappeared, we would die.

What is the food chain?

When you eat vegetables, meat, mushrooms, or any other type of food, you are gaining energy that comes all the way from the Sun. The energy gets into your food through a series of steps called the food chain.

Plants do not need to eat. They use the energy in sunlight to make their own food, which is stored as **carbohydrates**. This process is called **photosynthesis**. With energy from the Sun and nutrients from the soil, plants also produce **proteins**, **fats**, and **vitamins**. These things are stored in the leaves, stems, flowers, fruits, and roots of plants. Plants are the primary producers of food on our planet.

Next, animals come along and eat the plants. In addition to being tasty, plants provide the fuel and **nutrients** that animals need to grow and move. Animals that eat plants are called herbivores, or primary consumers.

If you dine on sizzling steaks, crispy chicken drumsticks, pork chops, or tuna, you belong to the next group of animals in the food chain—the secondary consumers. Secondary consumers receive some or all of their energy from eating other animals.

Secondary consumers are not at the end of the food chain. This spot is reserved for the **fungi** and tiny **bacteria** that feed on plants and animals once they have died. These organisms are called decomposers.

Plants draw energy and life from the Sun.

Primary consumers, such as cows and other herbivores, get their energy from the plants they eat.

BYTE-SIZED FACT

Herbivores are animals that eat only plants. Carnivores eat only meat. Omnivores eat both plants and animals. Carrion-eaters eat animals that have already been killed, or that have died naturally.

Snails, Insects, Beaver Tails, and Fungi— What Counts as Food?

Different cultures around the world consider different things to be food.

In France, large snails dipped in garlic sauce are a common item on restaurant menus. In some parts of China, chocolate-coated grasshoppers are popular. Beaver tails are skinned and fried in the Canadian Arctic. When you eat mushrooms on your pizza, you are eating fungi!

These things may seem strange, but they all count as food. They contain important nutrients your body uses to grow and stay healthy. So why does your stomach feel funny at the thought of nibbling on jellied moose nose?

What you are willing to eat depends largely on what you have been taught to think of as food. Tastes vary from culture to culture. They also differ from species to species. Humans are the only mammals that will not eat decaying food.

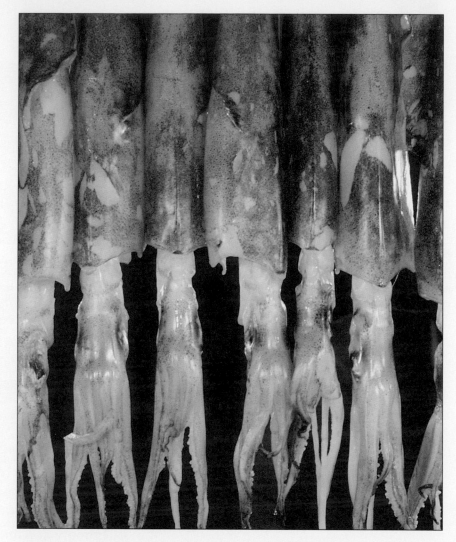

While many Western cultures would not consider squid a treat, it is eaten often in places such as Japan.

BYTE-SIZED FACT

Mushrooms are made of the same substance that makes up the outer skeleton of insects. It is called chitin.

Where did foods originate?

What you think is good to eat often reflects the plants and animals available in your part of the world. It takes time to get used to strange foods from far-off places. Europeans first came across tomatoes, potatoes, corn, and other New World crops about 500 years ago. At first they were not certain what to do with them. Can you imagine Italian food today without tomatoes, or Irish stew without potatoes?

Food was an important reason for the migration of Europeans to the New World. After tasting foreign spices for the first time, Europeans placed a greater demand on them. They sent explorers in search of quicker routes to India, the spice capital of the world. Along the way, these explorers discovered the New World, new people, and many new foods.

Over the past 500 years, New World crops, such as potatoes, have become staples of North American diets.

Without the introduction of tomatoes, we would never have tasted pizza, ketchup, or tomato sauce.

Old World Foods

apples	cherries	onions
asparagus	cucumbers	pears
beets	dates	peas
broad beans	figs	radishes
broccoli	grapes	spinach
cabbage	lettuce	strawberries
carrots	mushrooms	
celery	olives	

New World Foods

avocados	squashes
corn	sweet peppers
kidney beans	sweet potatoes
lima beans	tomatoes
pineapples	vanilla
potatoes	
pumpkins	
red peppers	

Where Does Food Come From Today?

Nearly 10,000 years ago, small groups of hunter-gatherers discovered they could add to their food supply by farming.

Farming gave humans crops and livestock as reliable sources of food. Today most people depend on ranches, farms, orchards, dairies, and fisheries to supply their food.

Take a brief look at these five major sources of food:

Ranches
When you think of ranching, you probably think of cattle roaming over huge areas of land. Today that scene is found mainly on television. Most ranchers raise their cattle in enclosures called feedlots, where hundreds of cattle live close together. This makes them easier to look after and to feed.

Farms
Like ranchers, farmers raise their pigs, chickens, or turkeys inside large barns. Outside, they grow vegetables or grains. Some farmers feed their crops to the livestock. Others ship their vegetables to market

Farming changed the way people lived and how they ate.

or sell their grain to companies that turn it into flour, breakfast cereal, or cooking oil.

Orchards
Fruit trees and nut trees grow in orchards. If you drive past a large orchard, you see thousands of trees spaced apart in rows. This prevents the trees from casting shadows on one another and makes it easier to harvest the crops.

You can pick fruit right off the branches at an orchard.

Dairies

Dairies raise cows, our main source of milk. Special machines milk the cows and pump the milk into cold storage tanks. The milk is then sold to companies that package it in cartons or turn it into butter, ice cream, or cheese.

Fisheries

Natural fisheries are areas of the ocean where, at certain times of the year, fishers catch large numbers of fish. Freshwater fisheries are ponds where baby fish are raised and harvested.

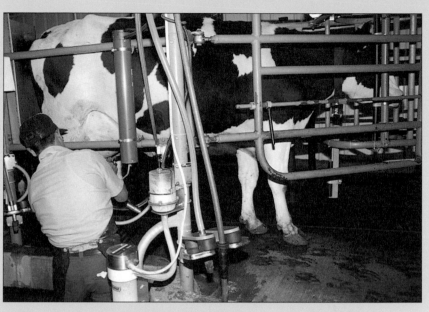

Cow milking is a high-tech operation, carried out with help from computers.

Fisheries supply us with tons of fish, which is eaten fresh or processed.

Here is your challenge:

Can you link the food in the left column to the plant or animal it came from in the right column?

FOOD	SOURCE
beef	cucumbers
dill pickles	soybeans
eggs	sheep
flour	pigs
ketchup	chickens
mutton	calves
pork	tomatoes
tofu	cattle
veal	wheat

ANSWERS:
beef — cattle
dill pickles — cucumbers
eggs — chickens
flour — wheat
ketchup — tomatoes
mutton — sheep
pork — pigs
tofu — soybeans
veal — calves

Genetically Altered Food

Would you eat potatoes that contain chicken **genes**? How about tomatoes that contain fish genes? Perhaps you have and do not know it. What is a gene, anyway?

Every plant and animal has a unique code inside each of its cells. The code determines what the cell does. A gene is a tiny bit of the code. It contains the instructions needed to carry out one task in the growth process.

Scientists look for genes that instruct the cell to do specific tasks. Some genes make things grow faster or bigger. Others help plants or animals develop a resistance to certain diseases or insects. Scientists transplant these genes into the cells of another plant or animal. The genetically engineered plant or animal may grow faster or bigger, or develop the resistance to certain diseases or insects.

Some people worry that genetically engineered foods may be harmful to eat. Others insist they are safe. Until we know one way or the other, should we label genetically engineered food? What do you think?

"The law does not require you to show the method a plant breeder uses to develop a plant." **Spokesman for the U.S. Food and Drug Administration**

"By not requiring labeling of all genetically engineered foods, the government is taking away my ability to assure customers the foods they eat at my restaurants are pure." **Restaurant owner**

"By the end of this year, millions of Americans will have eaten these foods, yet you won't be seeing anyone dying in the street." **Spokesman for the U.S. Department of Agriculture**

"The industry is depriving us of one of our most important natural defense mechanisms, reading ingredients." **Scientist at the Environmental Defense Fund**

How do you feel about eating genetically altered food?

What are calories?

There were probably dozens of **calories** in the last bite of food you ate. Do not panic. They will not hurt you, unless there are too many calories in all your food. Calories are simply the units we use to measure the energy in food.

Food energy is locked up inside carbohydrates, proteins, and fats, the three main nutrients in food. A gram of fat contains nearly twice as many calories as a gram of carbohydrates or protein. The trick is to eat the right number of calories to fuel your body every day. If you eat many more calories than your body needs, you gain weight.

If you eat too few, you lose weight. It is especially important for babies, children, and young people who are still growing to eat enough food. If people do not eat enough food, their bodies will not have enough fuel to work well and grow properly.

How many calories should you be getting in your diet? That depends on your age and how active you are. Growing teenagers and athletic adults need more calories than people who are less active. Your needs also depend on whether you are a male or a female. In general, males need more calories than do females.

Age (years)	Calories per day	
4 to 6	1,700	
7 to 9	2,100	
10 to 12	2,500	
13 to 15	girls	boys
	2,600	3,100
16 to 19	girls	boys
	2,400	3,600
Adults	women	men
	2,300	3,200

Packaged foods provide a label telling how many calories they contain.

BYTE-SIZED FACT

Food in the Body

"Is it time for dinner yet?"

Humans are not electric appliances. When you require more power, do you plug yourself into the wall or install new batteries? Of course not! You eat. But how does your body know when it is time for a snack or meal? Your grumbling stomach may be insistent, but your brain is the real driving force behind your hunger. You taste, chew, and swallow your food, then forget about it as you go on with your day. What does your body do with the food once you have eaten it? Your stomach breaks the food down and mixes it up. Your intestines break it up into even smaller particles that are absorbed into your bloodstream. From there, the nutrients are sent all over your body.

What makes you feel hungry or thirsty?

Your stomach grumbles when you are hungry. Your mouth feels dry when you are thirsty. But do these sensations make you hungry or thirsty? No. It is your brain that tells your body it needs food or water.

A special organ in the human brain called the **hypothalamus** keeps track of nutrient levels in your blood. It does this job all the time, even though you are not aware of it. If the hypothalamus finds that there are too few nutrients in your blood, it sends out signals to the muscles in your stomach to begin moving around, or grumbling. The grumbling makes you think, "Gosh, I'm hungry!"

The hypothalamus also checks on the balance of salt and water in your blood. Your body loses water when you sweat or go to the bathroom. If your body loses more than about 1.5 cups of water, your blood becomes too salty. The hypothalamus signals your mouth to dry out, which makes you begin thinking, "Wow, I'm thirsty!"

The brain sends signals to the rest of the body to let us know we are hungry or thirsty.

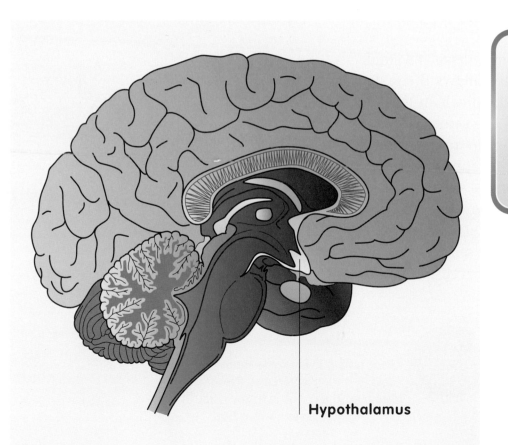

Hypothalamus

BYTE-SIZED FACT

You can fool your brain into thinking your body needs water by eating salty foods, such as potato chips.

How do you taste sweet, sour, salty, or spicy foods?

Taste is one of the five major senses. It is the way you tell which chemicals are present in food. Most foods that contain sugar, for example, taste sweet. Foods that contain poisonous chemicals taste bitter.

The four basic tastes are sweet, sour, salty, and bitter. Some people also include soapy and metallic as tastes.

Thousands of tiny taste buds on your tongue detect the flavors in food. Babies and children have far more taste buds in their mouths than do adults. This makes their sense of taste very powerful, so many children do not like too much spice in their food.

Saliva in your mouth dissolves small amounts of food. This allows the taste buds to detect the chemicals in the food. Different taste buds are sensitive to different flavors. Certain areas on the tongue are best at detecting each of the basic tastes. The tongue senses sweetness best at its front tip. Saltiness is best detected along the front edge, and sourness along the sides. Bitter flavors are tasted most across the back of the tongue.

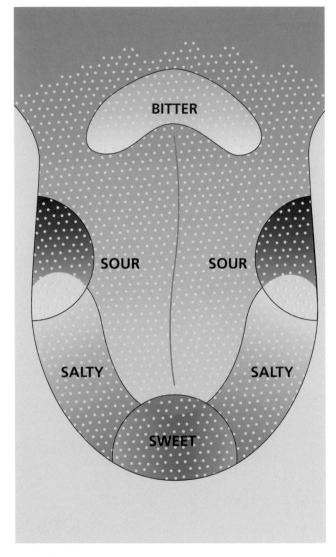

Different tastes are sensed more strongly from different areas on the tongue.

BYTE-SIZED FACT

Each taste bud lasts only about ten days. It is then replaced by a new taste bud. This comes in handy if you burn your tongue on something hot.

What happens to food in your stomach?

Food's trip through the human body begins in the mouth. First, chewing breaks food into small pieces. Next, saliva in the mouth begins dissolving the food.

When food arrives in the stomach, it triggers the stomach muscles to begin squeezing and crushing. At the same time, the stomach acid goes to work to help dissolve the food. In total, it takes about four hours for the stomach to mash up a meal and send it along to the next stop, the small intestine.

The small intestine is a long, coiled tube. The inside of this tube is lined with cells that act like guards. They allow only food nutrients to pass into the bloodstream through the wall of the small intestine. Anything that cannot be absorbed and used moves along and leaves the body.

It takes about four hours for the stomach to digest food and send it to the intestine.

BYTE-SIZED FACT

Chewing food into small pieces helps your stomach digest a meal faster. The acid in your stomach can attack and dissolve small pieces of food faster than large pieces.

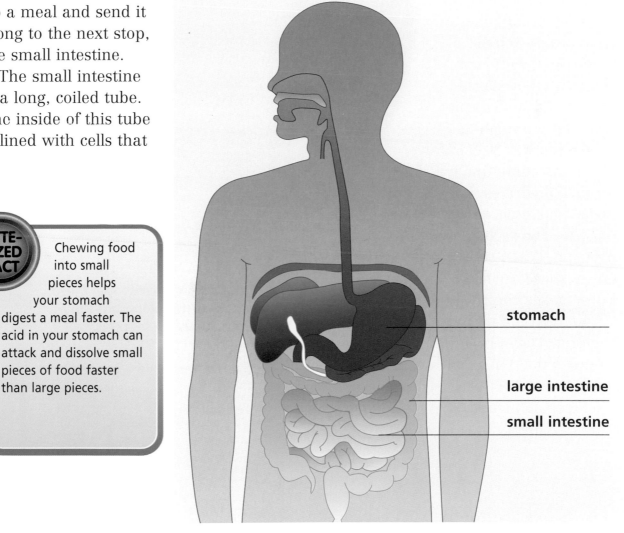

stomach

large intestine

small intestine

What lives inside our insides?

We are not alone! A person's intestine has millions of tiny, one-celled organisms called bacteria living inside it. The intestine is the long tube that leads from the stomach to the outside of the body. Digestion of food takes place there.

You did not have these bacteria when you were born. Where did they come from? You ate them along with your food, and they stayed in your intestine as the food went through it.

Two types of bacteria live in the intestine. One type feeds on carbohydrates. It gives off water and a gas called carbon dioxide. The second type feeds on proteins. When proteins are broken down, there are smelly gases left over. These gases contain nitrogen and sulfur.

You must not try to get rid of these bacteria. They produce important vitamins that your body needs in order to work properly. These friendly bacteria also keep some harmful types of bacteria from making a home in your body.

Seen through a microscope, these bacteria look harmless, but they can cause illness in humans.

BYTE-SIZED FACT

Herbivores must eat a great deal more than carnivores to get the same amount of energy and nutrients. For this reason, they have longer intestines to hold and digest more food.

What causes food poisoning and food allergies?

Harmful bacteria that live on food, kitchen surfaces, and utensils can cause food poisoning. These germs are too small to see, yet they can make you very ill. More than 40 million cases of food poisoning happen every year, resulting in up to 9,000 deaths.

There are several steps you can take to avoid food poisoning: Do not buy damaged food or food in damaged packages or cans. Do not leave cooked or refrigerated food at room temperature for more than two hours. Keep your hands, food, and cooking area clean. Cook food all the way through at a high enough temperature to kill the bacteria. If food looks suspicious, throw it out!

Some people are allergic to certain foods. When they eat that food, their **immune system** mistakes the food for a disease and tries

Care must be taken when handling and preparing raw meat. You can become very sick if meat is not cooked properly.

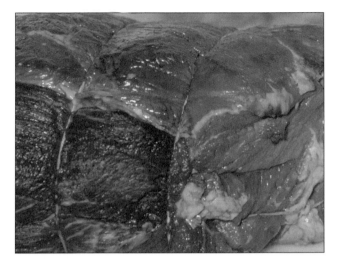

to destroy it. As a result, these people break out in a rash, get sick to the stomach, or develop a stuffy nose. Some people even die. Many people with food allergies may react negatively to the following foods: milk, eggs, peanuts, tree nuts, soy, wheat, fish, or shellfish.

BYTE-SIZED FACT

Peanuts are not nuts at all—they are legumes, like peas and beans.

Being allergic to peanuts is quite common. As tasty as they are, peanuts can make some people very ill.

Nutritionists

Are you curious about the nutrients in your food? Do you like to invent new recipes or plan what your family is having for dinner?

You could be a future nutritionist. A nutritionist is a person who knows exactly which nutrients are in every type of food. With this knowledge, a nutritionist decides which foods should be eaten for good health.

Most nutritionists learn about foods and food nutrients in college. After graduation, many nutritionists work in hospitals and clinics, creating diets for patients with special nutritional needs. Nutritionists also work for food manufacturers, inventing appealing, healthy food products.

Nutritionists help keep us healthy through proper diet and nutrition.

BYTE-SIZED FACT

Nutritionists advise us to eat food from each of the five major food groups every day. The five food groups are grains, fruits, vegetables, milk and milk products, and meat and meat alternatives. Ideally we should eat 6 to 11 servings of grain products, 3 to 5 servings of vegetables, 2 to 4 servings of fruit, 2 to 3 servings of milk products, and 2 to 3 servings of meat or meat alternatives. Meat alternatives include things like fish, eggs, and dried beans.

What are vitamins and minerals?

Carbohydrates, proteins, and fats are the sources of calories in food. Food also contains nutrients that do not provide energy. These nutrients are called vitamins and **minerals**. Your body must have vitamins and minerals in order to work properly. If you do not eat enough of any one vitamin or mineral, you can become sick.

There are several different vitamins and minerals your body needs in order to function. Each vitamin has a long chemical name. To make it easy, we call them by letter names, such as A, B, C, D, E, and K. The minerals are sodium, potassium, calcium, phosphorus, sulfur,

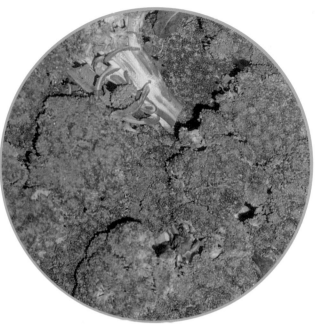

Both broccoli stems and flower buds are eaten. This vegetable is high in vitamins A and C and in calcium.

and magnesium. Your body also needs small amounts of the minerals iron, iodine, copper, fluorine, zinc, manganese, and cobalt.

Each of these vitamins and minerals helps with a different set of tasks inside your body. For example, vitamin A helps your eyes work better in dim light, and along with vitamins C and E, may help prevent cancer. Calcium helps build strong bones and healthy teeth.

Easy to peel, tasty mandarin oranges are a good source of vitamins A, B, and C.

BYTE-SIZED FACT

There are eight different B vitamins. All of them help the body convert carbohydrates, proteins, and fats into energy.

Food Facts and Myths

Do carrots help you see in the dark?

Carrots are rich in vitamin A, which plays an important role in sight. You must have some vitamin A in your diet in order to see well, but you do not need much of it. In other words, eating heaps of carrots will not improve your vision. If you did not eat any vitamin A, your eyes would have difficulty adjusting to low light.

Does spinach really make you stronger?

If you have seen Popeye® cartoons, you might think that a can of spinach will do wonders for your muscles. The iron in spinach gives Popeye® great strength. Spinach does have a bit of iron in it and a lot of vitamin A, which is good for you. But spinach does not have the same effect on people as it does on cartoon characters.

While spinach will not make your muscles bulge, it will help keep your insides strong and healthy.

Eating more carrots may help you see better in dim light.

Can an apple a day keep you healthy?

The apple is not a magical food that guarantees health, but it is very nutritious. An apple is a good source of fiber. Fiber helps food move through your intestine. And the apple peel is loaded with vitamin C.

Why is garlic good for you?

Scientists have found that garlic can ward off harmful bacteria, fungi, and **yeast** that make you sick. In fact, some people believe that eating raw garlic is as effective at fighting infection as common antibiotics.

Some people believe that eating garlic can prevent sickness.

Is it dangerous to eat green potatoes?

Potatoes turn green when you leave them out in the light for too long. Light causes potatoes to produce chemicals beneath their skin. One of the chemicals is **chlorophyll**, the substance that gives plants their green color. Chlorophyll is harmless, but in potatoes, it is associated with poisonous chemicals called **glycoalkaloids**. Peeling away the green part of the potato also gets rid of the poisonous part.

Apples are a good source of vitamin C and fiber.

Making Food Taste Good

"This is wonderful! I must get your recipe!"

Since our days as prehistoric humans, we have discovered many different ways to prepare food. We cook it, chill it, and spice it up. We mix different foods together to make stews, soups, breads, and casseroles. We even know how to use **microbes** to change one type of food into something different. A good example of using microbes is the way we change milk into cheese. Today, grocery store shelves are stacked with a variety of food products, and cookbooks are packed with delicious recipes.

Why do we cook food?

Many foods, such as sushi, carrots, and apples, are often eaten raw. Why are other foods, such as pork and potatoes, not eaten raw?

There are a few good reasons. The first reason is safety. High temperatures kill bacteria and other pests in our food that can make us sick. High temperatures also destroy some poisons.

Cooking also makes tough foods softer. This means they are easier to chew and digest. Just imagine trying to sink your teeth into a raw turnip!

Finally, cooking increases the flavor of some foods. It does this by heating the tiny **molecules** that are responsible for a food's flavor.

Some food is not cooked at all. Chefs use raw fish and vegetables to make sushi.

Here is your challenge:

Cooking sometimes changes the flavor of food. Try eating a piece of raw onion. Note the strong taste. Now eat a piece of onion that has been fried until it is browned. How does it taste? Sweet? High temperatures change some of the molecules in an onion so that they become 50 to 70 times sweeter than sugar!

What happens if food is overcooked?

Your older brother was talking on the phone and forgot the pizza he was heating in the oven. It is overcooked. Are you interested in eating it? Is it safe to eat?

The heat of an oven removes moisture from food. If left in the heat for too long, the food becomes dry and tough. High temperatures also destroy some of the nutrients in food.

Your pizza may be less nutritious and rather unappealing, but it is safe to eat. Now, what about those awful overcooked peas you ate at dinner last night?

Like the pizza, overboiled vegetables can lose both their appeal and their nutritional value. If you boil a vegetable for too long, heat breaks down the molecules that create the vegetable's flavor. Also, many of the vitamins originally in the vegetable end up in the water. Your overcooked peas were probably tasteless, mushy, and lacking in vitamins, but they were safe to eat.

Some overcooked food is not safe to eat. The black portions of burned food, especially burned meat, should be tossed in the garbage. They contain chemicals that may cause cancer.

Heat from a barbecue removes the moisture from hamburgers. If left to cook too long, they will become dry and lose their flavor.

How Do Microwave Ovens Cook Food?

Microwave ovens do their work by passing a special type of radio wave through your food.

Like radio waves, **microwaves** are invisible. But instead of carrying sound to a radio, microwaves in your oven affect the tiny molecules in your food.

Microwaves flip some of these molecules back and forth so quickly that they rub against one another and create heat. The molecules that flip-flop are called polar molecules, because one end has a positive charge, and one end has a negative charge.

Water molecules are polar. Water is an important part of many foods and makes them cook well in microwave ovens.

Have you noticed that the air in a microwave oven and the dishes you use in the microwave do not heat up? They are made of molecules that are not polar. Microwaves ignore these non-polar molecules. If your dishes are hot, they have been heated up by the food they hold, not by the microwaves.

Can you remember cooking without a microwave oven? Microwave ovens have become nearly essential in today's kitchens.

BYTE-SIZED FACT

Microwave ovens can flip over the tiny molecules in food up to 5 billion times per second.

What is food chemistry?

There are many chemical reactions that take place in our food and drinks. These reactions make it fun for us to prepare and eat certain things.

Why does soda pop fizz?

Soft drinks sit in a bottle or can, looking like any other liquid. But when you open the lid, thousands of little gas bubbles pop out of nowhere. Where did the bubbles come from? At the soft drink factory, carbon dioxide gas was dissolved into the soda pop liquid under great pressure. The liquid had to be very cold for this to work. When the container is opened, the high pressure inside is removed, and the gas escapes in the form of tiny bubbles.

Carbon dioxide is what makes our noses and throats tickle when we drink soda pop.

Why do chopped onions make your eyes water?

When you peel, chop, or crush an onion, you break open little pockets of special chemicals. When these chemicals are in the onion, nothing happens. But when they get loose and mix in the air, they can be unpleasant. One group of chemicals changes into two other chemicals: One causes your eyes to water. The other causes the strong smell of onions.

Onions release chemicals when they are cut. This is what makes you cry.

What makes gelatin turn from liquid to solid?

Gelatin is a popular dessert. It is made up of stringy protein molecules. When you dissolve gelatin in hot water, these strings uncurl and wiggle around.

As the liquid cools, the strings run out of energy to wiggle and end up sticking to one another. This creates a solid, three-dimensional net of gelatin strings that traps the flavored liquid inside.

Oil and vinegar do not mix easily. You must shake the bottle before the two will combine.

Why does salad dressing need to be shaken well?

Salad dressing is made of salad oil and a water-based liquid, with some herbs for flavor. Oil and water do not mix well. While sitting on the shelf, the salad oil stays separate from the water-based liquid. When you shake the salad dressing, it breaks up the oil into tiny droplets. The water-based liquid flows around these oil droplets, and you end up with a tasty mixture of the two.

This jiggly dessert goes through many changes as it cools into shape.

What makes popcorn pop?

Every kernel of popcorn contains moist **starch**. This is covered by a hard outer layer. When you heat popcorn, the moisture inside turns to steam, and the kernel explodes and turns inside out. The soft starch poofs out, and the hard shell ends up at the center.

Popcorn turns inside out before we can enjoy it as a movie-watching treat.

What are fungi and enzymes?

Some of the foods we eat are made with tiny organisms called yeast. Yeast produces special chemicals called **enzymes**. Among other things, enzymes help turn milk into cheese, make bread rise, and create alcoholic beverages.

Yeasts are very small fungi. There are about 160 different kinds of yeasts. The helpful yeasts that we use to make bread and wine are called "sugar fungi." We feed them sugar and, in return, they produce gas and alcohol. Baker's yeast creates more gas than alcohol, so we use it to make bread dough rise.

Yeast that creates more alcohol than gas is used for making wine.

Enzymes are proteins that speed up chemical reactions in food. Sometimes this is desirable, sometimes it is not. For example, enzymes speed up the chemical reactions that make fruit ripen and turn sweet. But the enzymes do not know when to stop. They go right on working until the fruit turns brown and soft. Likewise, enzymes help turn milk into cheese, but the cheese should be refrigerated to stop the enzymes from reacting further.

Bakers use certain kinds of yeast to make their bread loaves rise.

BYTE-SIZED FACT

Just one enzyme makes almost 1 million chemical reactions happen every second.

How is cheese made?

There are nearly 2,000 different kinds of cheese. Whether the cheese is made from goat's milk, yak's milk, or cow's milk, the same basic steps are used.

1. Color and special bacteria are added to the milk. The bacteria turn the sugar in milk into lactic acid, one of the chemicals that gives cheese its flavor.

2. An enzyme called rennin is added to the milk. This makes the milk form into a soft solid called a curd.

3. The curd is then cut into small cubes.

4. The cubes are cooked. They shrink and give off a watery liquid called whey.

5. The whey is removed.

6. Salt is added to the remaining curd.

7. Extra bacteria are added to some cheeses at this stage in order to ripen them properly.

8. The warm, wet curd is pressed into a form or bag. This squeezes out moisture and gives shape to the cheese.

9. The cheese is left alone to ripen, sometimes for several months. As the cheese ripens, the bacteria in it die.

Huge machines blend the ingredients used to make cheese.

Sealing machines ensure that packaged cheese stays fresh.

What happens when you make bread?

Have you ever watched bread dough rise? What is going on? Several steps need to be followed to make a loaf of bread.

Flour, water, and yeast are the main ingredients in bread. When you mix these together to form dough, some starch in the flour turns into sugar. The yeast feeds on this sugar, then begins to give off gas.

Next, you knead the bread. Kneading means folding the stiff dough over and pressing it together many times. This traps tiny pockets of air in the dough. The more tiny air pockets there are, the finer the bread's texture will be.

Now it is time to leave the bread alone and let it rise. During the rising stage, the yeast creates more gas. The gas increases the size of the tiny air pockets and makes the dough grow to twice its size. You punch the dough down, shape it into loaves, and let it rise again.

Finally, you bake the bread. The high temperature kills the yeast and keeps the dough from rising further.

Bakeries draw people in with the delicious smell of fresh breads and rolls.

BYTE-SIZED FACT

Most of the flavor in bread comes from the crust. Bread with a dark crust has more flavor than bread with a light crust.

Professional Baking

Do you like the feel of dough? Are you an early riser? Does the smell of freshly baked bread raise your spirits? Do you delight in decorating holiday cookies?

If so, you might be cut out to be a baker. A baker is a person who works in a bakery making breads, muffins, cakes, cookies, and pies. At home, you might make one or two loaves of bread or a few dozen cookies. A baker sometimes makes hundreds of bread loaves or thousands of cookies at a time. The baker operates special machines that process large amounts of dough. These machines do it quickly. A bread-making machine in a bakery can make dough that is ready for baking in only four minutes.

To become a professional baker, you must take courses at a technical school, and then work as an apprentice in a bakery for several years. You must also learn to get up before dawn. Bakers start work very early to have fresh-baked goods on the shelves when the bakery opens.

It takes a great deal of practice to make a perfect pie.

Bakers get up very early to make the fresh bread we find on store shelves every morning.

Keeping Food Fresh

"Get that moldy peach out of here!"

Nearly one-fourth of all food produced around the world is never eaten—at least not by humans. Insects, bacteria, and rodents get to it first. It is important for food that does come our way to remain fresh until we are ready to eat it. It needs to be protected from becoming bruised, crushed, dried out, spoiled, or covered in mold. To do this, people have invented special ways to package, prepare, and store food.

How do you keep food from spoiling?

Do you eat it all right away? That is one solution, but there are others. The cool temperature inside your refrigerator slows down the chemical changes that cause food to go bad. Cold temperatures also slow down the growth of tiny microbes, such as bacteria and fungi, that spoil food. Your freezer is even more effective. It turns the water inside food to ice. This completely stops most spoilage.

Heat works to prevent rotting as well. In a process called canning, food is sealed inside tins or glass jars. These containers are then heated until all the microbes inside are dead. This is important. If any microbes remain alive, they begin to grow again once the canned food cools off.

Hot and cold temperatures are only two weapons against rotting. There are others. The trick is to prevent harmful

Keeping food in the refrigerator can help it last longer by slowing down the growth of microbes.

microbes from growing. Drying takes away the water that microbes need to grow. Preserving uses sugar or salt to remove water from microbes. When there is a high concentration of salt or sugar on the outside of a microbe, water that is inside the microbe moves out. This causes the cell to die. When pickling, vinegar is added to food so that microbes cannot grow.

Microbes cannot survive in dried fruit because there is not enough water for them to grow.

Ripe fruit is in the earliest stage of rotting.

BYTE-SIZED FACT

Why keep air away from food?

Take a look inside your lunch bag. Does it hold a sandwich, or maybe a bunch of carrot sticks covered in plastic wrap? Have you ever wondered why the wrapping is necessary?

Imagine that you left a part of your sandwich lying around unwrapped. Would you want to eat it the next day? Probably not. The air slowly causes the moisture in the sandwich to evaporate. It shrivels up and becomes hard.

The air that passes over food also leaves behind **contaminants**. Contaminants are fungi and bacteria that grow on food and cause it to spoil. The tiny spores that start the growth of mold, for example, are contaminants that come from the air.

Chemicals that cause odors travel through the air and can be a problem. Uncovered food sometimes absorbs unpleasant-smelling chemicals from the air.

Food that is left unwrapped will start to grow mold and spoil.

A hard peel protects oranges against damage and spoiling.

BYTE-SIZED FACT

Some food comes in natural wrappers. Banana peels, pea pods, and walnut shells are just a few examples.

Why Do We Package Food?

Every home in every city throws out garbage every day. Our garbage contains things such as potato chip bags, ice cream containers, and used plastic wrap.

Using disposable packaging may seem wasteful. In some cases it is. In other cases the packaging is the only thing that protects the food inside from becoming too bruised and rotten to eat. There are four main reasons to package food.

First, some food is made up of very small pieces that need to be kept together. Imagine trying to carry rice home from the grocery store if it did not come in a bag or a box.

Second, delicate food bruises, breaks, and goes bad if it is dropped or bumped. This type of food can be safeguarded by covering it with protective packaging. An egg carton is a good example of protective packaging.

Third, light has a negative effect on some foods. For example, certain vitamins in milk are destroyed when exposed to light. Note how milk cartons keep light out.

Finally, in many cases, it is important to keep air away from food to prevent it from becoming contaminated by chemicals and microorganisms.

Even though it is important to protect food with packaging,

Waste products pile high at landfill sites across the country.

Small foods, such as pasta, must be sold in packages.

you can reduce the amount of garbage that you throw out. Choosing foods with as little packaging as possible and recycling what you can will help keep our planet clean.

Here is your challenge:

Look at the types of food in your home that come in boxes, cartons, bags, and bottles. For each type of food, can you identify one or more reasons that packaging is needed?

POINTS OF VIEW

Is Irradiated Food Safe to Eat?

Irradiated food has been exposed to high-energy radiation for 20 to 30 minutes. The radiation stops the growth of anything that is living in the food, such as harmful bacteria or insects. It also slows the decay of fruits and vegetables.

Irradiated food does not become radioactive. However, some people do not want to eat food that has been near radiation. Other people worry that workers who grow, handle, and package food destined for irradiation are not careful. They might leave dirt and insects on the food, knowing that radiation will kill any germs before the food goes to market. Who wants to find a dead worm in their apple?

Today, 39 countries around the world, including Canada and the United States, approve the use of irradiated food.

"The government approval of irradiation to destroy bacteria on red meats is a victory for consumers and the red meat industry."
President of the American Meat Institute

"Approving irradiation is like saying, 'Don't worry about how clean the packing house is, kill the germs, but maybe leave the dirt on the food.' That's not what Americans want."
Spokesman for the Center for Science in the Public Interest

Irradiated food no more becomes radioactive "than your teeth become radioactive by the dentist X-raying them."
Spokesman for an irradiation plant

"Today food flies in on airplanes after being sprayed with chemicals, irradiated, and genetically altered. It's enough to topple the Jolly Green Giant...or give him cancer."
Author of a book on organic foods

How do you feel about eating irradiated food?

Space-Age Food

Eating in space is a real challenge. Food does not just sit on the plate. Instead, it floats all over the place because there is no gravity to hold it down.

Although it may be fun to eat food in midair, food on the loose can be dangerous. It can get into the controls and experiments aboard the spacecraft. Liquids are especially a problem. If turned loose, they form tiny droplets that float around and eventually coat everything with a damp layer.

Astronaut food is packed very carefully. Complete freeze-dried meals travel in plastic bags. At mealtime, astronauts add hot water, stir the contents around, and eat right out of the bags.

Astronauts living in space will eventually try to grow their own food. Experiments show that space crops should grow best under tiny red and blue lights, not the glaring white lights used in greenhouses. Red light is particularly good at helping plants convert carbon dioxide and water into carbohydrates.

BYTE-SIZED FACT Astronaut Shannon Lucid took several flavors of gelatin powder packed in plastic bags onboard the *Mir* space station. For a treat, she just added hot water and put the bags in the refrigerator.

Space travelers rely on specially prepared freeze-dried foods.

Science Survey

What are your eating habits? Are you eating the right amount of good, nutritious food every day? The American Dietetic Association has conducted surveys about young people's eating habits. The association has asked questions to find out how often young people eat and what they eat. The survey results might surprise you.

What are your answers?

1. Do you eat breakfast?

2. Do you have dessert with lunch or dinner?

3. Do you eat candy and chocolate often?

4. Do you eat fish and poultry more often than beef and pork?

5. Does your daily diet include foods from all five food groups?

Survey Results

The eating habits of most young people over the age of 6 need improvement. Although many children choose low-fat foods over high-fat ones, they still eat too much fat. A major source of this fat comes from desserts. Also, more than 1 youngster out of 10 skips breakfast. This is a bad habit that can harm performance at school. Many teenagers get less than two-thirds of the vitamins and minerals they need daily. Forming habits like these can lead to heart disease, cancer, obesity, and diabetes later in life.

Desserts such as doughnuts are a major source of fat in young people's diet.

Here is your challenge:

Imagine you are given the job of planning the meals for your family. What foods will you provide?

Plan a menu for one day using the five major food groups discussed on page 20. List all the foods you intend to serve at each meal. If you want snacks between meals, include them on your list.

Fast Facts

1. One rotten apple does spoil the bunch. A rotten apple lets off a gas that signals the other apples to ripen and rot faster.

2. Bananas should not be stored in the refrigerator. They turn black if they get too cool.

3. You can determine a cranberry's freshness by bouncing it on the floor. The higher cranberries bounce, the better they are to eat.

4. Never use fresh pineapple chunks in your gelatin. Enzymes in fresh pineapple prevent gelatin from turning into a solid. Canned pineapple does not have the same effect. The enzymes have been destroyed by the canning process.

5. Our hunter-gatherer ancestors used thousands of plant and animal species for food. The agricultural revolution limited our diet to about 50 animal species and 600 plant species.

6. One pound of fat contains enough calories to supply the energy needs of an average person for 1.5 to 2 days.

7. While our taste buds are confined to our mouths, fish have taste buds all over their skin.

8. If the small intestine of an average human were split open and laid flat, it would cover an area roughly the size of a football field.

9. Raw pork sometimes contains tiny worms that can kill people if eaten while still alive. Thorough cooking kills the worms and makes the pork safe to eat.

10. It takes 2.6 gallons (10 l) of milk to make just 2 pounds (1 kg) of cheese.

11. Avocados will not ripen until they are picked. Instead of storing picked avocados, growers leave the avocado fruits on the trees.

12. The enzymes used in making cheese break down fats and proteins into smelly molecules. These are the same molecules that cause feet to smell.

13. Freeze-dried foods packaged in cans can be kept on the shelf at room temperature for up to 10 years. If they are packed in a plastic container, they will last from 6 months to 3 years.

14. About 500,000 tons of food products and ingredients are irradiated in countries around the world every year.

15. During colonial times popcorn with sugar and cream was served for breakfast. During modern times popcorn was the very first food to be cooked in a microwave oven.

16. On average each person in North America eats about 66 pounds (30 kg) of sugar every year and more than 11 pounds (5 kg) of chocolate.

17. Air pressure affects cooking. If you live high in the mountains, water comes to a boil faster. Cake batter flows over the edges of the baking pan if the ingredients are not adjusted.

18. Brown sugar is not healthier for you than refined white sugar. It is simply a mixture of white sugar and molasses.

19. It is probably a myth that Marco Polo introduced spaghetti to Italy following his travels in China. Italians had already made foods containing pasta, such as lasagna, macaroni, and ravioli.

20. Drinking 6 to 8 glasses of water every day is good for you. Water dissolves the food you eat and makes digestion easier.

Young Scientists@Work

Test your knowledge of food with these questions and activities. You can probably answer the questions using only this book, your own experiences, and your common sense.

FACT: The energy in food is measured in units called calories. Foods that contain fats, such as butter, meat, chocolate, and vegetable oil, have more calories than other foods.

TEST: Which one of these foods has the most calories? Which one has the fewest calories?

an apple

a chocolate milk shake

a raw carrot

a bowl of oatmeal

a candy bar

Answers: A chocolate milk shake has 420 calories. A raw carrot has only 20. The candy bar has 270 calories, the oatmeal 150, and the apple 60.

FACT: Many foods "go bad" if they are left uncovered.

TEST: Do an experiment to discover the best way to keep bread fresh. Cut a slice of bread into four pieces. Put one piece uncovered on the kitchen counter. Place another piece in a sealed plastic bag and set it next to the first. Now put one uncovered and one sealed piece of bread in the refrigerator. Wait one week. **Do not open the plastic bags at the end of the experiment. Throw them in the garbage.**

PREDICT: Which piece or pieces will still be good enough to eat? Look back to page 36 if you need a clue.

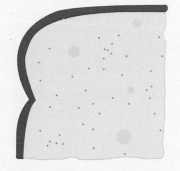

**bread slice # 1
(kitchen counter)**

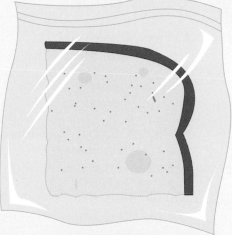

**bread slice # 2
(in plastic bag on kitchen counter)**

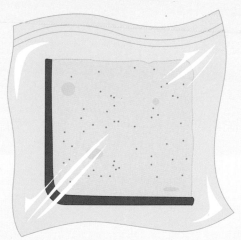

**bread slice # 3
(in plastic bag in refrigerator)**

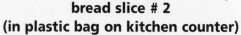

**bread slice # 4
(refrigerator)**

Research on Your Own

There are many places to find out more about food. Your local library, cooking schools, and the Internet all have excellent resources and information for you. Here are some awesome food resources to try:

Great Books

Creasy, Rosalind. *Blue Potatoes, Orange Tomatoes*. San Francisco: Sierra Club Books for Children, 1994.

Mandell, Muriel. *Simple Kitchen Experiments: Learning Science with Everyday Foods*. New York: Sterling Publishing, 1993.

Moore, Carolyn E., Mimi Kerr, and Robert Shulman. *Young Chef's Nutrition Guide and Cookbook*. New York: Barron's Educational Series, Hauppauge, 1990.

Nardo, Don. *The Encyclopedia of Health: Vitamins and Minerals*. New York: Chelsea House Publishers, 1994.

Ventura, Piero. *Food: Its Evolution Through the Ages*. Boston: Houghton Mifflin Company, 1994.

Great Websites

The American Dietetic Association
www.eatright.org/child/

Kids Food Cyber Club
www.kidsfood.org/

The Popcorn Institute
www.popcorn.org/mpindex.htm

Glossary

bacteria: Tiny, one-celled organisms. Some bacteria help digest food, and others can cause diseases.

calorie: The unit used to measure the amount of heat energy in food

carbohydrates: Sugars and starches

chlorophyll: A green pigment found in green plants that absorbs energy from sunlight. Plants use it to make food and oxygen.

contaminant: A substance or organism that pollutes or infects

enzyme: A protein that speeds up chemical reactions

fats: The organic oils and grease in foods

fungi: Plantlike organisms with no roots, shoots, or leaves. Mushrooms and molds are examples.

gene: A unit of information that controls one characteristic of an organism. Genes are passed along from parent to child.

glycoalkaloids: The poisonous chemicals in potatoes that make them green

hypothalamus: An organ inside the brain that regulates hunger, body temperature, mood, and sleep

immune system: The body's defense against disease

microbes: Living organisms too small to see without a microscope

microwaves: Electromagnetic waves 0.04 inches (1 mm) to 20 inches (50 cm) in length that are used to heat food in microwave ovens

minerals: Certain solid elements that the body uses in tiny amounts to build and maintain its various parts

molecules: The smallest particles of a substance, composed of one or more atoms

nutrient: A substance, usually an ingredient in a food, that the body needs to grow and remain healthy

photosynthesis: The process by which plants make sugar from water and sunlight

proteins: Large molecules made up of long chains of units called amino acids. The body needs proteins to function properly.

starch: A type of carbohydrate found in plants, especially potatoes and cereal grains such as rice and wheat

vitamins: Organic substances the body uses in small amounts for maintaining good health

yeast: Tiny fungus cells that reproduce very quickly when grown with sugar

Index